Why LDS Should Support Black Lives Matter

(Note this conversation was recorded on Jan 28, 2021. The interview has been lightly edited for clarity.)

Introduction

As we approach the Juneteenth celebrations (the real end of slavery in the United States), I thought it would be good to talk to Loki Mulholland. He is an Emmy-winning filmmaker, author, activist and son of civil rights icon, Joan Trumpauer Mulholland. His work has received over 40 Telly Awards and his films on race and social justice issues have won 20 Best Documentary awards. His first book, "She Stood For Freedom" was nominated for the 2017 Amelia Bloomer Award. Loki's film, "The Uncomfortable Truth" won an Emmy in 2018 and has been viewed over half-a-million times on Amazon. Loki is a member of Omega Psi Phi Fraternity, Incorporated and speaks all over the country on issues of race and social justice. He is the founder and Executive Director of the Joan Trumpauer Mulholland Foundation which was created to end racism through education. We'll talk about why Latter-day Saints should support Black Lives Matter. Check out our conversation...

Tags: Gospel Tangents, Rick Bennett, LDS Church, Latter-day Saints, LDS Church, Mormon, Mormon Church, Church of Jesus Christ of Latter-day Saints, Mormon history, Mormon, LDS Church, LDS, Church of Latter Day Saints, race & LDS Church, Loki Mulholland, Joan Trumpauer Mulholland, racism, End of Slavery, Black Lives Matter, After Selma, voter suppression, Black White & Us, Darron Smith, Joan Trumpauer Mulholland, Black Lives Matter; After Selma; voter suppression; Black White & Us; Darron Smith, The Evers, Uncomfortable Truth, After Selma, Black White & Us, End of Slavery, An Ordinary Hero, apology, LDS priesthood ban,

Contents

End of Slavery (in Utah???)

Introduction

Did you know slavery was still legal in Utah until 2020? We'll talk about the drive to remove this provision in the Utah Constitution with an Emmy-award winning director, Loki Mulholland who directed the film "The End of Slavery." Check out our conversation....

Interview

GT 00:14 Welcome to *Gospel Tangents*. I'm excited to have an Emmy Award winning director here. Could you go ahead and introduce yourself to our audience?

Loki 00:22 Well, I'm Loki Mulholland. I'm the executive director and founder of the Joan Trumpauer Mulholland Foundation. I make films and speak and write books and all that sort of stuff on social justice issues.

GT 00:38 Yes.

Loki 00:39 I'm the son of Joan Trumpauer Mulholland, which our foundation is named after. She's a civil rights icon.

GT 00:46 And your mom.

Loki 00:47 And my mother, yeah, that's true. I forget about that sometimes.

GT 00:52 (Chuckling) This is exciting. I've known Loki for 15 years.

Loki 00:57 Yeah.

GT 00:59 We were actually in the same ward.

Loki 01:01 Yeah.

GT 01:03 Loki has his own podcast. Why don't you tell us a little bit about that?

Loki 01:06 Oh, yeah, *The Uncomfortable Truth*.[1] The podcast talks about race and racism in America. It's titled after the Emmy winning film that we did called *The Uncomfortable Truth*,[2] as well. It's Luvaghn Brown, who's a freedom rider African American, what is he like 70, now, and myself. So, it's a black guy and a white guy having the conversations that usually don't take place. We just kind of go through all that. Season one was really kind of dialing in on race and racism in America. It's season two right now. We're doing interviews with some of our friends, who are civil rights activists, people like Ruby Bridges,[3] and Dave Dennis, Jane Elliott and the like.

GT 01:48 Cool. It's pretty fun. We've known each other for a long time. You actually started out making other films that were not documentaries.

Loki 01:59 *Believe*.

GT 02:00 So, give us give us a little thumbnail sketch of what *Believe* is about.

Loki 02:03 *Believe* is a mockumentary about network marketing. It's a satire about the multilevel marketing industry.

GT 02:11 I'm trying to remember...

------

[1] You can listen to the podcast at https://podcasts.apple.com/us/podcast/the-uncomfortable-truth/id1498323248

[2] You can watch the movie at https://amzn.to/2RGoa7B

[3] The episode is available at https://tinyurl.com/LokiRuby

Loki 02:12 It was good times.

GT 02:13 I'm trying to remember, your main character was it Lincoln Hoppe?

Loki 02:16 Lincoln Hoppe, yeah. He is going to be in the new film, The Witnesses.

GT 02:22 Oh, okay.

Loki 02:23 He plays Martin Harris, I believe.

GT 02:25 He was in the Singles Ward[4] before that.

Loki 02:26 He was in Saints and Soldiers.[5] He's been in those and a lot of other shows and stuff.

GT 02:33 It's a funny movie. My family fell in love with it. I know it didn't get a lot of play in the theaters, but it's a funny movie. Go look it up, *Believe*. It's pretty funny.

Loki 02:44 I actually did an interview. I probably shouldn't say the name. But I did an interview at a network marketing company, a job interview for video production. The first question they had when the door was closed, it was like, "Are you the guy who made *Believe*?" I'm like, "Yep." I'm sitting there going, "Yeah, I'm not getting this job." The guy kind of looks around, even though doors are the closed, he's like, "Yeah, we thought was great. We loved it." I'm like, "That's great. Right on. I'm not getting this job."

GT 03:17 That's hilarious. I hadn't heard that one before. Well, tell us about your latest project.

---

[4] See https://amzn.to/3oINxSs
[5] See https://amzn.to/3wkIR7O

Loki 03:23 My latest project is called the _End of Slavery: the Fight for Amendment C_.[6] It's about the fight to actually take the language of slavery out of the Utah State Constitution. When the Utah State Constitution was written, they actually wrote in the language of the 13th Amendment, which was that slavery is abolished, except as a punishment for crime for those who've been duly convicted. What that means is that you can be re-enslaved again, not you and I, but African Americans, because that's what it was written for. So, that was created as a nod to the South to re-enslave people, to put them into penal farms, and then do convict-leasing. So, what they would do is, if you were African American, you could be arrested for something like loitering. Loitering meant that you didn't have a job and you were just kind of hanging around. Well, the problem was, is that white people weren't going to hire black people. So, you couldn't get a job. So, now you get arrested. You're put into a penal farm. You're leased back out to the mines, to the railroads, to the farms, to the plantations, and worked like a slave all over again. This is all part of the black codes and everything.

GT 03:26 It's not just picking up trash on the side of the road.

Loki 04:33 No, it's not just picking up trash on the streets, not things like you think about today. But, that was really the start of the jailing institutions that we have today. It was just another way, not only to re-enslave people, but also to take away the right to vote. Voting is power and African Americans, at that point, had the right to vote, but we need to take that away from them. So, that became, also, part of that whole system. What was interesting was, Utah was founded 30 years after slavery ended. The Civil War was done and everything. Yet, for some reason, they wrote that in there. So, Sandra Hollins, she is the first black female elected official in the State of Utah. Right now, she's the only black elected official in the state of Utah.

GT 05:27 We've got Burgess Owens, technically.

---

[6] See https://amzn.to/2TpuFwb

Loki 05:29 But, he's not a state official.

GT 05:31 Okay. He's a federal official.

Loki 05:32 He's a federal official. This was brought to her by a reporter who said, "Hey, did you know this was still in here?" Colorado had already passed this. Utah is not the only state that had this in their state constitution, but they took it out in Colorado. So, they're like, "Wow, we need to do this here in Utah." So, a couple of years back, I think I want to say it was 2019 or so, 2018, 2019, the bill was passed in the House, which is where she is, and then it went to the Senate the next year. Then, it was on the ballot for the State of Utah to vote whether to take it out or not. The interesting thing I thought when I was making the film, was that in the State Capitol, I wanted to get a shot of Sandra standing in front of the Constitution. We'd rack focus from her to the Constitution, like chiseled on the wall. I don't know why I thought would be chiseled on the wall or something. But there was no copy of the Constitution anywhere in the Capitol Building. I'm like, "Well, no wonder why no one knew that was there."

GT 06:34 So it's hard to find the Utah Constitution.

Loki 06:36 Yeah, it's like, in a vault down underneath the Rio Grande archive.

GT 06:44 We always hear about the senators that have their little pocket Constitution of the United States.

Loki 06:49 Right.

GT 06:49 Why do we not have that more available here in Utah?

Loki 06:53 That's above my paygrade. It's another film, I guess. Out of sight, out of mind.

GT 07:00 So, people just didn't know it was there, didn't know it was still there?

Loki 07:04 Well, yeah, I think for the most part, they really didn't know that was there. I mean, there's so much stuff that's in the Constitution. But, more importantly, this is not like one of those laws that people wrote, like 100 years ago that you can't bring a bear into church, because someone did that and mauled everyone. So, those were sort of funky things. I think, in Louisiana, you're not allowed to chain an alligator to a fire hydrant. There are laws like this. But this is, obviously, a lot more meaningful. This was written in the Constitution. The only logic anyone has that it was written in there was because Utah wanted to become a state, and polygamy was a big issue. So, they're trying to say, "Hey, look, we really want to be Americans," whatever that means. So, they basically just took the U.S. Constitution and its amendments and threw it right into theirs, and just went about their merry way. The idea is like, "Oh, gosh, well, we're not going to have slavery again." I actually said that to someone, "It's not like we're actually really going to have slavery again." She goes, "Yeah, but words have meaning. Those words weren't written for you. They were written for me."

GT 08:21 It's interesting. So, I was lucky enough to watch your film. The one thing that I think is interesting to me, is--because you just focus on the year 2020. It took us until 2020 to actually abolish slavery completely in Utah. But how familiar are you with like the 1852 Act in Relation to Service? Do you have a lot of background on that?

Loki 08:51 For Utah?

GT 08:52 For Utah.

Loki 08:52 No. I do know that slavery existed in Utah, even prior to when it was even a territory. This region, the Mexicans were enslaving Native Americans and so forth. So, there's a long history to all that in and of itself. I'm not up on the 1852 stuff. I'm really focused on the current history.

GT 09:13 Yeah, I know Paul Reeve is coming out with a new book on the 1852 legislature.[7] The interesting thing is, that's when Brigham Young asked the legislature to legalize slavery, which, of course, lasted from 1862 until the Emancipation Proclamation, was that 1864, I believe?

Loki 09:31 Yeah. 1863-64.

GT 09:32 Civil War period.

Loki 09:35 But, the Emancipation Proclamation didn't free anybody.

GT 09:39 Only in the south. That's right.

Loki 09:40 Only in the south. It only applied to those people who were enslaved in rebel-held held territories. So, people in Delaware, Pennsylvania, Maryland, they were still enslaved.

GT 09:54 Well, I think in Pennsylvania, they had an emancipation law that predated the Civil War, if I remember right. It was kind of a gradual emancipation, but, yeah, but it was still technically legal in the northern states. I guess--neither one of us are real history experts. But it was soon after the Civil War when...

Loki 10:17 I'm a history expert.

GT 10:18 Okay.

Loki 10:18 Just not that part of history.

---

[7] See our interview at https://gospeltangents.com/2017/02/09/how-mormons-became-a-racial-category/

GT 10:22 So, we have the 13th amendment.

Loki 10:25 Yeah, the Reconstruction Amendments were 13th, 14th, and 15th.

GT 10:27 Okay. That's when we finally abolish slavery nationwide.

Loki 10:32 Right, now, it didn't actually end until December of 1865, when it finally passed the final state, cleared the barriers. Now, technically, not every state signed that off, or if they did, they forgot to mail it in. Like Mississippi, for example, didn't end slavery. Technically, slavery didn't end in Mississippi until like, 2014, or something. It's a little ticky-tack. We're getting a little [picky] there. But, the fact of the matter is, there was a clerical error. So, what does that mean?

GT 11:11 It's interesting that a lot of these slave states in the South tried to keep slavery alive through the penal system. It's interesting to me that Utah, in a nod to the south...

Loki 11:24 Now, let's hold on. Let's be clear on this. The United States kept slavery alive in the South.

GT 11:33 Okay.

Loki 11:34 Because this was the United States, this wasn't the southern states. This wasn't the Confederacy anymore. When they rejoined the union, and had to sign off on those amendments, the United States government decided that keeping that language and that amendment was important enough to allow for the re-enslavement of African Americans. Now, it might not have been chattel slavery, like we had in the past, but it was still slavery. That was the federal government's decision, not the state's decision. That was the federal government.

GT 12:03 Can we blame that on Andrew Johnson more than Abraham Lincoln?

Loki 12:03 Well, Abraham Lincoln was dead. Yes. So we can definitely blame it on Andrew Johnson. Andrew Johnson, you have to understand, was just a horrible, horrible individual. Even his addresses to Congress and stuff, and this is all documented, because this is like a State of the Union address. I mean, he's literally saying, all this sort of language about that blacks are inferior, and slavery was good for them and all that sort of rhetoric you hear, because, why? Because, well, he was an enslaver. He was definitely down for the southern cause.

GT 12:38 Yeah. It's too bad Lincoln picked him. I know he wanted to have a unity government, so he tried to pick a Southern Democrat on his ticket.

Loki 12:48 Kennedy did the same thing with Lyndon B. Johnson, to balance that Yankee ticket, because he knew that, guess what? The southerners aren't going to vote for Catholics, or a Catholic president. I mean, there were lynching Catholics in the south, good grief, along with African Americans and Jews, and probably a Mormon or two.

GT 13:09 Yeah. There's an interesting book about Joseph Standing,[8] who was a missionary in Georgia, that was lynched. There's a building in the MTC[9] named after Joseph Standing. I actually stayed there when I was in the MTC. I need to interview the author. She's not Mormon. She talks about Joseph Standing's life.

Loki 13:31 None of us are Mormon. We're Latter-day Saints. Let's be clear on this.

---

[8] Can be purchased at https://amzn.to/3hNWqsx
[9] Missionary Training Center in Provo, Utah.

GT 13:33 (Chuckling) That's right. But anyway, it's interesting that slavery was technically abolished, but yet we have the Jim Crow laws in the south. Why does Utah like to tie with Southern laws such as this one here where, it's okay. We can still have slavery as a punishment. That was actually put in the Constitution.

Loki 14:08 Well, I think, at the end of the day, it was just a matter of just to kind of appease the Union in and of itself. It was because, "Hey, look, we want to be part of this country. We want to be a state in that respect and it's just basically throw anything and the kitchen sink in there. Let's allow our constitution to look like the U.S. Constitution." They just threw that in there. I mean, it was kind of like, "Hey, we're not of bunch of crazy polygamous radicals and so forth. We're Americans." I think more than anything, it was just optics. However, the fact of the matter is that they felt that it was okay to put that in there to begin with. They didn't have a problem with that. Not every state has that. Right now, I think there's maybe like nine states that have that in their constitution. Colorado, again, was the first one to clear that out. It took them twice to actually do it.

GT 15:07 Oh, really?

Loki 15:08 Yeah, so Utah, hey, it only took us one time. Colorado, it took them twice. Oregon's working on that. They're next in line.

GT 15:15 A northern state.

Loki 15:16 Yeah. Nebraska, I think, [did it at] the same time that we were doing it, so in 2020, they did it as well. But yeah, no one really has a clear answer as to why that's in there. Except, again, I just kind of go on optics, more than anything else.

GT 15:34 Interesting. Are you aware of any history of people being enslaved after statehood in 1896, as part of this penal system?

Loki 15:47 No.

GT 15:49 So, it was just more of window dressing than anything.

Loki 15:51 Right. The fact of the matter is that exists there, and the same systems that the South was using could be applied here. Racism existed here. It still does, as a matter of fact, in case anyone's wondering.

Loki 16:07 It's part of the attitude, part of the lens through which they saw things. No one that could make those determinations, thought it was a bad thing to have in there, "We don't see anything wrong with this." Of course not. It doesn't impact them. I think that was kind of the bigger part of the film, in and of itself, was to help people understand why does this matter? Well, it doesn't matter to someone like me, because it's not going to impact me. That would be the general attitude. We don't have to think about it as white people. But Representative Hollins and her constituents here in the state, particularly African Americans looked at and went, "Oh, my gosh. This is scary." All this stuff adds up. It's just one more thing. Well, if we don't need to have it, then let's get it out of there. Of course, [some people say,] "Well, what about the cost, " and this and that and this. What about the cost? You tell me what the price of a human life is.

GT: I know that you interviewed some people in the documentary that were like, "I voted no."

Loki: Yeah, we have a couple of got people like that. It's interesting. I think it ended up being about 20% voted against the law.

GT 17:29 Against repealing slavery.

Loki 17:30 Against repealing slavery in Utah. I think that some of them didn't even know what they were reading, didn't even know how to interpret what they were reading. Maybe when they said no, they meant, "Yeah, I'm against slavery." Some people don't even bother reading stuff, it's just a blanket sweep, boom, done. Now, there are those, like a couple people that we interviewed, who were just like, "I'm opposed to this. Where does it where does it end?" I think it's pretty impressive that only 20% voted against it, given the climate at the time that we had during that election. We just went through the summer with Black Lives Matter. It's not a very popular thing here in Utah, amongst a certain set of people. There's a lot of back and forth on that. So, you're going through all these emotions and everything else, and here's one more thing. For a lot of white people, particularly here in Utah, they see something like that, and they're just going, "My gosh, man. What else do they want? Aren't they happy enough?" They, meaning African Americans, of course. So, the fact that only 20% [opposed it,] remember, Colorado, the first time they did it, it didn't pass. So, go Utah!

GT 18:57 It didn't pass the legislature or didn't pass the vote?

Loki 19:02 It didn't pass the vote. Not enough people voted for it in Colorado. The second time, it finally passed.

GT: That's weird.

Loki: Part of it was the language and how they phrased it and so forth. That's my understanding. But the fact of the matter is, if you know how to read, then you should be able to understand what's being said. You had people in the film, one person talks about that this is like, "They want to take away our guns." This has nothing to do with the Second Amendment. You should have heard what else he said, after that. I didn't put it in the film. He went off about Pelosi and this and that. He was talking about all sorts of Q Anon type stuff. I was saying, "Oh, my gosh." The other person was just like, "Well, I mean, I thought we already had slavery here. I mean the IRS takes all your money."

GT: I remember that.

Loki: I'm like, "Okay, whatever." It wasn't like we were cherry picking those responses. Those are the two people who are willing to talk to us. Then we were at a voting place. They allowed us to interview people and we had to jump a lot of hoops for that. But we had interviewed four or five people and we only used a couple. It's a short film. We didn't want everything to just be interviews. One guy was a Mexican American and other guy was Korean American. We wanted a different viewpoint.

GT 20:16 Well, let me throw this idea at you. We think of chain gangs now. We think of prisoners picking up trash on the freeway. Is that a form of slavery?

Loki 20:29 That's the big question. That was a question that was brought up of how that rehabilitation aspect of incarceration [would be affected.] That was actually put into legislation, because that was a concern that they wouldn't be allowed to do that, to provide those services for rehabilitation, whatever that's supposed to mean.

GT 20:50 So, picking up garbage is considered a form of rehabilitation?

Loki 20:54 Apparently, so.

GT 20:55 So, that's still okay to do.

Loki 20:57 Right. But the thing is, even in Utah, and a lot of states, you have situations where incarcerated people are being paid pennies on the dollar, to make products for corporations. I've talked to several people about that, even here in Utah, not in the film, but they're like, "Hey, by the way, did you know that this, this and this?" I'm like, "Oh, my gosh, I had no idea it was that bad." So it's like, "Well, yeah, well, they're getting paid." Okay, but, in California, when the wildfires [were burning,] they were taking incarcerated people to go fight fires. That's a pretty dangerous job, and you're only paying them like, what a couple bucks, right? The capitalist argument to that would be, well, if you're paying them $2 to fight a fire, whatever it is, then you're not going to pay the other guy 30 bucks, because look, I've got cheaper labor. So, now it's just a matter of taking advantage of people and now you're suppressing the labor force anyways, for those sorts of things. It's exploitation, at the end of the day, because you have a group of people that really don't have a say in the matter. If you don't want to do this, then state yourself, whatever it might be. But there is an exploitation factor in that. I can get into private prisons as well, if you want me to. The problem with the private prisons and all that is that literally these private prisons have sued states for not having enough prisoners. These are public companies that trade on Wall Street. So, in their filings, their whole formula is about having more prisoners. So, they go and actually lobby Congress to find ways to imprison more people, to change up laws, to make things more strict, to stay longer in prison, because why? Because they get paid by the state to incarcerate people.

GT 22:51 Then they can lease out their prisoners to do essentially under minimum wage jobs. I mean, there's a thought out there, why would slavery not be okay for prisoners? Because we're here to punish them and this is punishment.

Loki 23:11 But that's not what prison is for. Prison is for rehabilitation, not punishment.

GT 23:18 I think a lot of people would disagree with you on that.

Loki 23:20 Of course they would. Yeah, I understand that. But the way it's pitched is that this is about "they have to do their time." We understand doing the time for the crime. But we want you to come out a better person. You've learned your lesson. You've paid your dues to society, and come out a better person. If you're being exploited, and so forth, that's not really the whole point of all of that. To think that they don't know that is pretty ignorant in and of itself.

GT 23:51 There are some people who complain that, "Oh, well, this person got a bachelor's degree while they were in prison, and I can't get a degree. Why are we paying to educate prisoners?" What do you think about argument?

Loki 24:05 It's cheaper. For tax purposes, it's cheaper to educate someone than it is to incarcerate someone, plain and simple. They have done studies on that.

GT 24:16 That was in one of your other movies.

Loki 24:18 It wasn't in my film.

GT 24:19 Wasn't it in your film?

Loki 24:20 That was in Waiting for Superman.[10]

GT 24:23 Oh, that's right.

Loki 24:24 Yeah. But there's actually studies that are done on that. To actually pay for four years of college, I think in *Waiting for Superman*, it was all about private school for these kids, and then pay for college. It was like, four years of that was cheaper than one year of them being incarcerated.

GT 24:42 Yeah.

Loki 24:43 You have to understand the economics of that again. We're a capitalist society. So any capitalist would appreciate this. If I'm incarcerating someone, they're not paying taxes. I'm paying for them to be in there. But, if someone is a productive member of society, who's gone to school, who's getting high wages, guess what? They are paying taxes. So, they're adding to society, not

---

[10] See https://amzn.to/3yuReQb

subtracting from it. So, you want more people to add to society. That's just the way it should be. I mean, look. We are not the Soviet Union here. This is not communism. We don't just throw people in the gulags, even though we've incarcerated more people than China. So, what does that tell you? Nonetheless, for all those arguments against socialism, well, gee, a prison system that pays people 15 cents or whatever to make Gucci watches. I am exaggerating, but that's more socialist than anything else. Yes, I'm getting a little political here. I know the arguments. Are you sure you want this interview? (chuckling)

Son of a Civil Rights Icon

Introduction

Joan Trumpauer Mulholland began protesting for civil rights in the early 1960s and was part of many of the important civil rights protests of the decade. Her son Loki has become an Emmy-award winning director and in our next conversation, we'll talk about why he made a film about his mother's activism. Check out our conversation….

Interview

GT 25:46 Well, let's talk about some of your other films. Actually, let's also talk about how did you get involved in in civil rights and that sort of thing?

Loki 25:56 What's your first question?

GT 25:57 Well, let's go with that one. How did you get involved in civil rights, first?

Loki 26:01 How could I not?

GT 26:03 A lot of people don't.

Loki 26:05 A lot of people's mothers aren't Joan Trumpauer Mulholland. They don't have statues of their mothers and museums and her mug shot is considered one of the most famous in American history.

GT 26:14 I'm sure a lot of my listeners probably aren't going to know who your mom is. So, tell us a little bit about your mom.

Loki 26:20 By the time my mom was 19 years old, she had been involved in about three dozen sit ins and protests when she joined

the Freedom Rides and was put on death row. That's the beginning
of her story. She's kind of the Forrest Gump of civil rights. She was
everywhere and knew everyone, from Fannie Lou Hamer to Dr.
King, Jackie Robinson. Actually, I learned more about my mom after
I made the film than I did during making the film, because there's
new stuff that comes out all the time.

GT 26:49 Yes, so you're talking about *An Ordinary Hero*.[11]

Loki 26:50 *An Ordinary Hero*. Yes. I'm sorry. Yeah. So, the
documentary that I did about my mother called, *An Ordinary Hero*,
which is about her life in the student movement of the civil rights
movement. When she was 10 years old, she went to Georgia
where her grandmother lived, the southern grandmother. Every
summer they would go there. When she was about 10 years old, on
a dare, her and her friend go to the black quarters. Of course, they
had a different name for it then. She saw the discrepancy in the
living situations, but in particular, the schoolhouse. So, the
schoolhouse is like classic, straight out of Hollywood, one room
schoolhouse for black children, with no glass in the windows, no
paint on the walls. [There was] a potbelly stove in the middle, for
heat, an outhouse. This is in stark contrast to the brand-new post-
World War II brick building, that was in this little town for the white
students. Now that building is still the nicest building in Oconee,
Georgia. It's now just a rest home for, probably for all those
students, [who were there] 70 years ago. So, she sees this, and she
says, "This is wrong. I've got to do something about it." She actually
said that it rattled her soul, because of what she was taught in
church. My mom's Presbyterian. [She was taught] that we do unto
others as you would have them do unto you. "If you've done it unto
the least of these, my brethren, you've done it unto me." She says
all of that good King James stuff. She really took that to heart.

Loki 27:01 She had to memorize the Declaration of Independence,
that all men are created equal, and she really believed it. "The

---

values of what our country espouses," she said, "We're just not living up to them." So, when she sees this for herself, for the first time, for real--we can see things all the time, but when it finally registers, I guess, is the point. [She] kind of connected the dots. All of a sudden, it became, "Wow, this is wrong." She gets her chance. My grandmother decided. When my mom graduated from high school, and she wanted to go to a small, kind of church school in Ohio, which is where her Sunday school teacher went, which was John Glenn, the astronaut. My grandmother was just aghast. She was like, "Oh, no, what if she has a classmate who's black, or heaven forbid, a roommate who's black. I'm going to send her to Duke."

GT 29:21 Because Duke had no black students?

Loki 29:24 Duke was segregated. It was a safe school, which was the worst place to send her if you want to keep down the civil rights movement, because just down the road was Greensboro, North Carolina, which is where the first student sit in took place with the Greensboro Four on February 1, 1960. The next sit-in was in Durham. My mom was invited to join, and as they say, "The rest is history."

GT 29:49 And there's a famous photo.

Loki 29:50 Yeah.

GT 29:51 With her getting [food dumped on her head.]

Loki 29:52 Well, that was a few years later.

GT 29:54 Oh, that was a few years later, okay.

Loki 29:55 Yeah, I did have some photos, my mom but not that particular sit-in.

GT 29:59 Was that [photo of] the Woolworth Lunch Counter?

Loki 30:01 Right. That's the 1963 Woolworth's Lunch Counter, Jackson, Mississippi, where they poured the stuff on her head, and there's Ann Moody and John Salter and a mob of two or three hundred people behind them. I can probably count on my hands the number of times my mom has said, "That's when I thought we were going to die." I found out later, she was, actually, on the Klan's most wanted list, and was actually hunted down for execution. But, because they failed, they ended up killing a couple of her friends, instead.

GT 30:29 Oh, wow. That's terrible.

Loki 30:34 My mom's pretty cool. I get people who ask me all the time, "Well, would you sit at the lunch counters?" I'm like, "Well, I don't have to. My mother already did. But I have to do what I can do, because doing nothing is not an option."

GT 30:51 So these films are kind of your lunch counter.

Loki 30:54 Films are my lunch counter. Right. It's my way of continuing that process of healing and educating and moving the work forward to help us actually form that more perfect union, to go back to the principles of who we are as a nation, of who we want to be as a nation. We've gotten better. We honestly have. I mean, good grief. We don't have slavery anymore. We don't have Jim Crow anymore. I mean, we actually had a black president. We have a black Vice President. That's progress. It doesn't mean that there's still not that foundation of racism that we still need to work on, that each of us need to work on. There's something to be said, when President Oaks is saying Black Lives Matter, when the First Presidency is very open about race and racism in America, and within the Church, and how we should be living as members of the Church, as well. I mean, you can either take the buffet approach to the gospel and pick what you like, and so forth and ignore the rest.

The argument I've always heard is, "Well, they're just trying to be with the times." I'm like, "Okay, when has the First Presidency ever tried to be with the times?"

GT 32:13 (Chuckling) They fought against [ending] polygamy, [de]segregation?

Loki 32:16 Second of all, aren't they prophets for our time? So, yeah, right. The essay on race,[12] and so forth. I was there at a temple recommend interview, and the bishop said afterwards, "Is there anything I could do for you?" I said, "Yeah, I'm actually kind of curious as to why we haven't talked about the anniversary of the restoration of the priesthood for African Americans." I said, "How come we haven't talked about any of that? How come we haven't talked about the essay that the Church just came out with on racism?" He's like, "What are you talking about?"

GT 32:55 Most bishops don't know about the essays. I think it is getting a little bit better.

Loki 32:59 Yeah, but it was like, "Oh, I hadn't even thought about that." I'm like, "Well, don't we mourn with those who mourn?"

GT 33:08 Well, I had a conversation, since you just talked about Black Lives Matter, with my Bishop. I referenced Elder Oaks' talk about Black Lives Matter and his response was, "But not the group. The group's a Marxist organization. I'm like, "Black Lives Matter. I don't care about the group." How do you respond to people when they say, "But that group's a Marxist organization?"

Loki 33:39 Well, first, it's not. I think one of the leaders believes in some of the Marxist ideals, but let me ask you this. So, if a member of the Republican Party is a Q Anon follower and believes that

---

[12] See https://www.churchofjesuschrist.org/study/manual/gospel-topics-essays/race-and-the-priesthood?lang=eng

Jewish lasers are starting forest fires, does that mean every Republican is a Q Anon follower? Right? If, I can point to...

GT 34:02 We can paint [with a broad brush.] Because we do that with black organizations. They did it with Martin Luther King, that he was a communist. There's a picture with him sitting next to a communist, which was a staged photo[13] that people don't understand still.

Loki 34:15 Right.

GT 34:15 And the John Birch Society still loves to promote [that photo.]

Loki 34:17 Yeah, sure.

GT 34:19 So, it's easy to paint Black Lives Matter as a [bad organization.] It's just the same old [smearing campaign.]

Loki 34:24 Mitt Romney sits with Democrats. Does that make him a Democrat? I mean, come on.

GT 34:29 People would say yes. But yeah, so I love that, the Q Anon thing, because...

Loki 34:38 And I am Q, by the way.

GT 34:39 You're Q? (Chuckling)

Loki 34:42 If you don't know, then that's because you just don't know. So that's the beauty of Q.

---

[13] See our interview with Dr. Matthew Harris at
https://gospeltangents.com/2019/03/hoover-on-mlk-etb

GT 34:46 (Chuckling) So, yeah, we don't do that with white organizations like Q Anon. If we wanted to paint with the same broad brush with Black Lives Matter, as we did with the Republican Party, we could say, "Hey, Marjorie," whatever her name is, [Taylor Green] "represents the entire Republican party and Q Anon."

Loki 35:08 Right.

GT 35:09 So, yeah, I think that's a that's a great response there.

Loki 35:13 I mean, at the end of the day, the question becomes, why do they feel compelled to say that?

GT 35:21 To denigrate the cause.

Loki 35:23 Well, yeah, but I'm saying, why would African Americans feel compelled to say Black Lives Matter? Whether you agree with the statement or not because you want to politicize it and so forth, once you get to the source of the matter, not the what, but the why. One of our general authorities has said this. The "what" informs us, but the "why" transforms us. So do a gut check and ask why. Why do they feel compelled to say this? Well, it's because there are issues that are clearly played out almost on a daily basis of African Americans facing police brutality, right up to murder, and we know this, and we've seen this.

GT 36:02 The response is, "Well, they shouldn't have gotten arrested."

Loki 36:05 I actually said the other day in an interview. Someone was like, "Look, white people don't care if white people get killed by the police." We just don't care. The only time we care when someone gets killed by the police is if it's a black person, and black people are complaining about it. That's the only time we ever bring it up. All of a sudden, we have an issue because, otherwise, if a white person gets killed by the police, well clearly, they deserved it. But what we're finding out is that's not really the case. People aren't actually deserving it half the time, and no one deserves that anyways. What type of society are we that we say that people deserve to be murdered?

GT 36:42 You know, I look at Eric Garner. What was his capital crime?

Loki 36:46 Right, selling loose cigarettes.

GT 36:48 Yeah. I didn't know that was a capital crime, personally.

Loki 36:51 Right, that's grounds for murder? I mean, give me a break. If you actually believe the second great commandment, "Love thy neighbor as thyself," I think it is, whatever it is. I'm clearly not a scriptorian, guys. But if you truly believe in the Gospel of Jesus Christ, that we should love each other and treat each other the way we want to be treated, then that should be deplorable. There's no ambiguity in any of that. You should mourn with those who mourn.

Loki 37:25 I mean, to me, it's sad that we will run around as Latter-day Saints, white Latter-day Saints and say, when someone says something about, "Well, aren't you guys racist." We're like, "Well, hold on now. I mean, more than half our Church are people of color." That shocks people. We actually are. The majority of the members of the Church are actually not white. We love saying that because it makes us look good. It doesn't mean we actually care about them. Right? Not at all. Because the second one of our fellow Latter-day Saints that's not white says something that goes against that, that makes us question who we are, as Christians, and our fundamental beliefs. We've got issues. I did a post yesterday about Black Lives Matter and a member of my ward [commented,] "All lives matter, period." I'm like, "I'm unfriending you," because he does this all the time. I'm done. You're [about] 80 years old. I know exactly where you're coming from with this. I'm not going try to convert you or anything. But it's like, "Why would you say that?"

Loki 38:34 It was Fourth of July, it was the Genesis choir, the black Genesis group. It was their choir. They were singing at this Fourth of July thing. It was up near American Fork Canyon with the largest American flag ever to hang, that sort of thing. I go there. Genesis is a predominately black choir. I go there with a Black Lives Matter T-shirt. Yes, that was intentional. This lady next to me goes, "All lives matter." I said, "Well, I'm glad you agree that Black Lives Matter." That's not what I said. I said, "Well, you just said all lives matter, so if all lives matter, then you agree with Black Lives Matter. She just got in a huff and walked away.

Loki 39:17 Just think about what you're thinking about first. Try to think, first of all. But think about what you're what you're saying. This goes to like the heart of immigration and so forth. When the argument would be like, well, we shouldn't be putting people in cages. "Well, they shouldn't have come here illegally." Well, no one has ever said they shouldn't come here illegally. I've never heard anyone say, Democrat, Republican, anywhere say, "It's okay for people to come here illegally." It's how we treat people when they get here. Are we going to be like the Soviet Union and China and this North Korean stuff, or are we going to be America? If this is the greatest land on Earth, why do we think it's only good enough for us? If we think it's so great, we want everyone to be here. God created people, not borders. But, again, fundamentally, it's how we treat people when they're here, our own citizens, our own brothers and sisters in the Gospel. This is why the Church came out and said, "This is horrible." But, for some reason, we don't want to listen to the prophet as much as we want to listen to politicians or our neighbor, or whomever else that has regurgitating sound bites that they've heard from somewhere else.

GT 40:32 So, it does seem like politics is our new religion. We're getting a lot of pushback, especially among Church members.

Loki 40:40 You're not going to get a lot of likes on this interview, by the way.

GT 40:44 Well, it depends. I have a broad audience. Some will love it. Some will hate it, I'm sure, as that is the case with many of my interviews. Do you get a lot of push-back in the ward, then, with your advocacy for Black Lives Matter and things like that?

Loki 41:03 Well, not during not during COVID.

GT 41:08 (Chuckling.)

Loki 41:09 That's been nice. People are pretty much cowards. They're not going to say anything to me.

GT 41:21 It's easier not to be a coward on Facebook for some reason.

Loki 41:24 Right, yeah. I remember I got a message, and it wasn't anyone in my ward, I know that. I hope it wasn't. But people have said that I have absolutely hate for the white race, which is ironic. I've had someone say that someone should put a gun in my mouth to silence me. So, yeah, I get those sorts of threats and things like that, because the guilty take the truth to be hard. That is scripture, isn't it?

GT 41:50 (Chuckling.)

Loki 41:52 Wait, I do know, scripture. I'm a convert to the Church.

GT 41:57 Yeah.

Loki 42:00 My mom struggled with the idea of that, because she believed that Mormons were racist. Well, yeah, okay, not every Mormon. Well, guess what? So are Presbyterians and so are Catholics and so is everyone else.

GT 42:11 So, was she opposed to your joining the Church because Mormons were racist?

Loki 42:15 She was worried.

GT 42:16 Okay.

Loki 42:17 She wasn't going to tell me what to do, just like her parents couldn't tell her what to do. But John Salter, who is in that famous photo sitting next to my mom in the Jackson Woolworth's, he grew up in northern Arizona. He sent her a letter it said, "Joan," that's my mom, Joan. He said, "Nothing but good can come from this. I grew up with Mormons. They're good people." And, from that, is all the genealogy work that we've done since then, and whatnot. It's really kind of opened a lot of doors, and a lot of understanding for people and so forth. My mom has really been open about that point. Now, it's funny because I was in Alabama, at the, what was it? [It was] the Freedom Ride Museum in Birmingham. I was passing through on my way to Mississippi, from Georgia. So, I stopped there, just kind of popped in to say hello, and I'm chatting with the person who runs the museum. She knows who I am, because of my mom. I get that a lot.

GT 43:29 There's probably a lot more black people who know who you are than white people, I'll bet.

Loki 43:34 Yeah. As we're there, a friend of hers pulls up and she does tours and things like that. We're all sitting there talking to him, saying, "Hey, how's it going?" I didn't know who she was. Then she say, "So, where are you from?" Normally, when people say to me, where are you from, I don't say Utah, because I don't want to have that conversation. I can hide that because, I'm white. It's not like I'm Hispanic or something and all of a sudden, I can't hide anything. No one's going to ask me my religion. In polite company, you don't talk about those things. So, where you're from, so for some reason, this time, I said, "Utah."

She said, "You're wearing a Black Lives Matter T-shirt?" That was the perception of Utah. It still is.

Then the lady that was initially there with me says, "Don't you know who this is? This is Joan Trumpauer's son."

She says, "Oh my gosh, I had no idea. I'm so sorry."

I'm like, "No, I'm not offended." So, I'll get asked that. Are you Mormon? I'm like, "Yeah."

"Really?"

Loki 44:46 Actually, in our interviews for *An Ordinary Hero*, there's a famous photo of a burning bus in Anniston, Alabama from the Freedom Rides. They had bombed the bus on Mother's Day. They let church out early so people could bring their children to watch the Freedom Riders burn alive on Mother's Day. Happy Mother's Day. Let's watch people burn alive. This is the sick sort of stuff going on here in 1961. But we're interviewing Hank, and we flew him out here to do the interview. He goes, "So, are you Mormon?" I'm like, I want to deflect this. How do I? I don't want deal with it. I go, "Yeah, so is Danor." Now, Danor Gerald was one of our producers. He's an actor here and filmmaker and stuff. But he was there with me, and I go, "Yeah, so is Danor." He's African American. But, he goes, [to Danor] "Wait, you're Mormon?" He [Danor] goes, "Yeah, so is Gladys Knight." He goes, "What? Man, I just assumed all Mormons were racist." He literally had called his wife that night. He told me the next day. We're eating dinner and stuff. He's like, "Yeah, I had to call my wife and tell her. You ain't going to believe what I just heard. Gladys Knight is a Mormon."

GT 46:01 Yeah.

Loki 46:02 That changes everything. He was just like, he said, "I have to go home and tell people." Now, again. It doesn't mean that we've arrived and so forth, but as people have a greater understanding of who we are, and what we represent, and so forth, and that we're more than just a caricature to people. When they start interacting, they start to understand. I think that's one of our bigger problems, particularly here in Utah is we don't have that interaction. Our wards are lily white. Our schools are lily white, the majority of these places. So, we don't have that meaningful interaction that really needs to take place amongst different people, be it LGBTQ, or Hispanic or black or whatever. When you have those meaningful interactions, you can no longer just blatantly throw aside, something like Black Lives Matter, or immigration issues, because you understand. You feel for people. It's called empathy. More than anything, I think the Savior was the great empathizer. He could understand what everyone went through. He believes Black Lives Matter, so should we. And he proved it, because his prophets have said it.

GT 47:24 Interesting.

Films Combating Racism Directed by a Mormon

Introduction

The LDS Church has had a rough history when it comes to race, so it may surprise you to find out that one of its members has made several award-winning documentaries, including an Emmy dealing with racism. We'll talk about these award-winning films from director Loki Mulholland. Check out our conversation....

Interview

GT 47:25 Can you give us a rundown of your films that deal with racial issues?

Loki 47:30 Okay.

GT 47:31 We've talked about *An Ordinary Hero.* We've talked about the *End of Slavery.*

Loki 47:36 *An Ordinary Hero*, which is about my mom, and the student movement. Then, there's *The Uncomfortable Truth*, which is about the history of institutional racism in America, how we got to where we are. That's actually a genealogy journey, as well, very fascinating. I get messages from people asking me about--all sorts of questions about that film still.

GT 48:00 Well, and your family had owned slaves, right?

Loki 48:05 Yes, we owned people. Yeah. We actually helped start the whole thing, quite frankly. We arrived in Jamestown in 1610. We were one of the original planter elites. We served in the House of Burgesses. We were there. We also were one of the original signers of the Declaration of Independence. So, we're real Americans.

GT 48:34 (Chuckling)

Loki 48:35 I say that a little facetiously, but the fact of the matter is, I get people who tried to argue that I'm not a real American because blah, blah, blah. I'm like, "Hey, wait, hold on. Hold on one second, now. We fought in every war. Right? We did all of it. We did everything. We were there for all of it, the good and the bad.

GT 48:56 And that *Uncomfortable Truth* is uncomfortable.

Loki 48:58 It is. It should be. It's a dialogue, really. It's a perspective. You have me talking about my story. Then you have Luvaghn Brown, he's telling his story. Luvaghn Brown is black Freedom Rider who grew up in Mississippi, who didn't like white people. He didn't trust white people, particularly white women. My mom was the first white woman he ever trusted, because trusting white women back then can get you killed.

GT 49:26 Emmett Till.

Loki 49:26 Emmett Till is the classic example. Luvaghn Brown was 11 years old when Emmett Till was killed, and it was just right up the river in the delta of Mississippi. [It was] Money, Mississippi, as a matter of fact.

GT 49:37 Well, I know there's a new movie coming out on Emmett Till, with Devery Anderson. You and I both know Devery.

Loki 49:43 Yeah, Devery's great.

GT 49:44 Devery's the biographer of Emmett Till, basically, right?

Loki 49:47 Yeah, he basically wrote the Bible on Emmett Till.

GT 49:50 Yeah. Devery is LDS. He works at Signature Books.

Loki 49:54 He lives in Salt Lake. I have a documentary that I've been working on for a couple years about Emmett Till, as well with Devery and Jerry Mitchell and so forth.

GT 50:02 Oh, so, we've got two things to look forward to.

Loki 50:04 Yeah.

GT 50:06 Devery's got something coming up on ABC, if I recall.

Loki 50:09 Yeah, well, he's involved in it. They're using his book, and he's a consultant and all that.

GT 50:14 Yeah. Your movie is coming out on Emmett Till. Do you have any idea when that will be released?

Loki 50:20 No. I'd like to say this year. It was going to be this year, but there was still some stuff we had to shoot back in Mississippi and COVID destroyed all that. So, I've already done one edit. I did the first edit, which is the edit I kind of throw away, that tells me this is horrible. So, basically, here's how the film process works. You get a really great idea, you're like, "This is going to be amazing. This is going to be awesome." Then you shoot it, and you're like, "This is a train wreck. This is never going to work." You edit it., and then you're like, "Okay," and then you salvage something out of that. You make your film in editing as the phrasing goes. It's such a different film for me compared to my other ones.

Loki 51:02 So, the other ones, to continue that is, is "*Black, White, & Us,*" which is about racism through the lens of transracial adoptions in Utah. So, these were white families who believe that racism doesn't exist anymore, and then they adopt these black children. It's this eye-opening experience for them. Because now suddenly, their neighbors, their own family members, everyone else is coming out of the woodworks saying all sorts of stuff to them. But they actually have to confront racism, because these are their children. They can no longer sit there and go, "Yeah, but. Maybe that's not what the police meant when they pulled you over, and maybe this and maybe that. Maybe that's not what your teacher said." And it's like, "No, I mean, this is actually for real." It's a fascinating exploration. When I work with teachers, I tell them, "Look, you really need to watch this film, because the majority of teachers are white women. The majority of students now are people of color. So, there's a disconnect there. Of course, they say, "Well, these are my children. I love them." And rightfully so, teachers can say that, because they probably spend more time with our kids than we do. But, how well do you know your kids? This is the Brother's Keeper type thing.

Loki 52:15 Another film is *After Selma*, which is about voter suppression since the 1965 Civil Rights Act. So, Selma, Alabama, the Edmund Pettus Bridge, that has iconic images. People are like, "Oh, well, everyone can vote. All as well." Well, no, not all is well. There's still a lot going on. So, that's that film. Then, obviously, the "*End of Slavery*," and "*The Evers*." This is about the family of Medgar Evers, and his assassination. He was shot in the back by Byron De La Beckwith while standing in his driveway. We interview his wife and his kids and so forth. We have to understand that these historical places, actually. These people are still alive in a lot of cases when it comes to civil rights movement. These are real stories. These are real people, real lives, real impact. So, when you go and see their house where he was killed, it's not just merely, "This is an historical place." It's like, "No people lived here. They laughed. They loved. They cried. It's making history real. So, that's idea. But this Emmett Till film is a completely different style for me, and how I want to approach it. Because filmmakers, we get bored and we want to do something new and, so it's probably going to be a train wreck, because you should just stick with what you're what you're good at.

Loki 52:19 (Chuckling) So is it going to be a documentary style, or is it going to be more drama or...

Loki 53:44 No, it's documentary style, still, but just a different style of documentary than before. Then, I'm exploring a piece about American Indians, focus on Bear River Massacre, the Shoshone, and so forth. That's going to be another leap for me. We're looking to do re-creations and those sorts of things.

GT 54:05 I think I helped introduce you to Darren Parry.

Loki 54:07 You did, yeah. You helped introduce me to Darren Parry.[14]

GT 54:09 Darren's a great guy.

Loki 54:10 Darren is a great guy. Yeah. So, those, those are some of the things we're working on. We've got curriculum for kids that we do from our foundation. I do assemblies all the time with students, and speaking engagements and stuff. We're recording in February right now, so it's Black History Month. So, there's 19 school days in February, and I've got 19 assemblies. I think it's actually more than that now. I've got at least, gosh, I think eight. Just myself, I have like eight speaking engagements in February on top of all that. So, it just keeps getting busier and busier. We've got the podcast series and I've got another series that's called *Locked in with Loki.* If this is too hard for you, you're not going to want to listen to *Locked into Loki.* So, there's a lot there that we're just trying to, again, kind of coming back to that, how did I get involved in civil rights? Well, I say my mom, which is obvious, at that point, but it's just part of who I am. In my belief, like my mom, that we should all be treated equally. That's what our constitution and Declaration of Independence says. That's what the scriptures say. That's what our prophets say. My mom has said, "I can't do everything, but I can do something, because doing nothing is not an option." So, this is what I can do.

----

¹⁴ See our interviews at https://gospeltangents.com/category/darren-parry/

GT 55:41 Have you considered doing anything as far as racism within the Church?

Loki 55:46 No, not yet.

GT 55:48 Okay.

Loki 55:49 There was a film, a documentary I was going to do, but it just didn't come together, that was going to be called, "I am not your Mormon." Oh, that was a little play on, James Baldwin's, "I am not your Negro," which is actually not what he said. That's actually the polite form that they use to sell the movie, because he used the N word. But, yeah, so that was kind of this play on that a little bit, but it just hasn't materialized yet the way I wanted it to. And, yeah, I don't want to get excommunicated.

GT 56:22 (Chuckling)

Loki 56:25 Maybe things are better now that that wouldn't be the case, since we've got a great partnership with the NAACP and all the work we're doing with genealogy with the Freedman projects and so forth. I mean it's surprising a lot of people that the Church has come very much a long way in a very short time. The tone is set at the top. With all this sort of stuff that always goes on, the tone is always at the top, whether it be religious or political. It just takes a long time for it to trickle down. We saw that with polygamy, of course. But like we were talking earlier about the essays on race...

GT 57:01 Yeah.

Loki 57:01 It's like, suddenly, the bishops are like, "What, these things exist?" It's like, "How did you not know this? I mean, you're the bishop." Well, the bishop is human. There's so much being done and being said, within the Church at the top, that a lot of people just haven't figured out what all that means yet. The Church is working heavily with the NAACP right now. I mean, we funded several million dollars for the slave museum in South Carolina, one of the major slave ports was, I think, in Charleston or something like that.

GT 57:35 The Church did this?

Loki 57:36 The Church has a big part of that.

GT 57:37 I have not heard about that. I've heard about the museum, but I didn't know the Church had involvement with that. That's interesting.

Loki 57:42 We worked with the Smithsonian, that Freedman's Bureau project and stuff was with the Smithsonian at the African American Museum.

GT 57:49 There was the Freedmen Bank, too. I know that Richard Turley talked a little bit about how that is really helping black people with their genealogy, from that bank.[15]

Loki 57:57 That's a hard thing, genealogy for African Americans, because the records aren't there. So, you really have to piece stuff together in a whole different way. The DNA stuff that's going on nowadays has, I think, made a major leap as well. The Church is, actually, in Africa. So, a lot of stories, just like here with the American Indians and stuff, a lot of that's just oral history. It's not written history. But you have people in Africa, specifically, in these tribes, their whole thing is genealogy, orally. So, they can tell you like 13 generations back, type of thing, who everyone is. That's their whole thing. So, they're actually recording these guys, in these tribes, and documenting all of this, to help. So, when you start making those connections back to these tribes, then all of a sudden, now you can start to really to understand your family history, to bring the past the immortality and the eternal life of man.

---

[15] See our interview at https://gospeltangents.com/2020/12/hired-after-hofmann/

Loki 57:59 I look at what I do in that context with my kids, when they were young. I guess they'll always be young in my book, but anything you do in life, just make sure it's in harmony with what the Savior's doing and then you can't go wrong, whatever that might be. You could be a manager at McDonald's and still bring the pass the immortality and eternal life of man. It's how you interact with people. It doesn't matter what you do in life, just make sure it's in harmony with that. Racism is a sin. The Church has said that, and sin is separation from God. We know that. And God's plan is what? To bring to pass the immortality eternal life man. That is his one mission. So, if I can help people overcome that racism and see people as God sees them, that's really what I'm doing and that's what it's all about. Sometimes that means we have to clear out some of our own baggage, our own philosophies and so forth that we've been fed through family, through church, through media, through history books, whatever else. You need to get back to who we truly are as people.

GT 1:00:11 You've mentioned the essay a few times, what are your overall thoughts on the essay? Is it good? Does it leave out too much stuff? What do you think about that?

Loki 1:00:20 Just like with any essays, it's a balancing act. I think it's great, personally, just because the fact that we even have one. I think it's pretty clear about Brigham Young. It's pretty clear on a lot of these points, about the curse of Cain and that sort of nonsense and whatnot. To me, it's pretty unequivocal. Now, I'm a white guy saying this. I have to preface that. It's easy for me to say that, because I'm not living those experiences. That's we have to understand. I'm not living some of those experiences that other people can see, and go, "Wait a second." But I think they did [a good job.] They've put a lot of thought into it. There's always stuff that's cut out, for whatever reasons.

GT 1:01:06 I know Dr. Matt Harris, when I talked to him, because he was the one who critiqued the essay.[16]

Loki 1:01:11 Yeah.

GT 1:01:11 By chance, did you hear that interview?

Loki 1:01:14 No, I haven't heard that one, but we've talked about this before.

GT 1:01:17 One of the things that I mentioned to Matt, was the one thing about the essay is you can read it as, "Hey, God inspired the ban." That's one reading, or you can read it as, "No, it was all Brigham Young." Some people say, "Well, we've kind of thrown Brigham Young under the bus."

Loki 1:01:40 He deserves it.

Loki 1:01:44 I go the rounds with this. My mom said this the other day on a panel. I was like, "Oh my gosh, mom, really? Are you going to say this again?" So, my mom, she'll say, "I'm from Arlington, Virginia. Robert E. Lee was my homeboy." I'm like, "Really, mom? You're still saying this?" Understand, she grew up under that mythology of Robert E. Lee. She's 79 years old. She grew up in America, for goodness sakes. I mean, what else is she going to think? But you would think someone like her would kind of get over that. When you challenge her on that, she will give you some history of Robert E. Lee about his work in reconciliation and so forth, after the war. There's a lot that he did.

GT 1:01:45 He did not like slavery.

Loki 1:02:13 Well, he didn't mind benefiting from it. Now, my mother will tell you that, as well, "Wait a second. He actually gave his land to the enslaved people before he left the Union." It was the federal government that said, "You can't give it to them." So, I

---

mean, there's that. But also, he was a horrible person who beat
people to an inch of their lives. I'm talking about enslaved people.
He is a traitor. He did fight against the Union. Now, my mother
would say, "Well, look, back then, people didn't identify with the
country, they identified with their state." Okay, but the fact of the
matter is he went to West Point.

GT 1:03:12 Lincoln wanted him to be his general, and he turned
Lincoln down.

Loki 1:03:18 The point being is that, like with Brigham Young, yes,
we can see some of these aspects and go, okay. This is sort of the
cancel culture attitude type of thing, but people go, "You did
something horrible. Guess what? You're a horrible person." And
slavery was horrible. We know that. But do we also believe in
forgiveness? "I, the Lord will forgive whom I will forgive, but of you,
it's required to forgive all men." That's in Doctrine & Covenants. I
don't know where it is,[17] but I remember seeing that. That's my other
scripture. I cherry pick the scriptures I can throw out at people. But,
let's be honest, that's the facts. Can people change? Yes. There's
quite a bit of evidence of that beyond the scriptures, just in life.

GT 1:04:12 Even George Wallace.

Loki 1:04:14 Well, George Wallace changed the wrong way, by
the way.

GT 1:04:18 But didn't the end of his life, because you know, he got
shot. He tried to be a little bit more accommodative.

Loki 1:04:24 Yeah, definitely. But at the end of the day, it's like,
"Okay, where do we draw the line?" Are we going to forgive Hitler?
That's not our job. Well, I guess it is, according to the scriptures. But
he also didn't do anything redeeming, either. He went to his grave
wanting to kill all the Jews.

---

[17] D&C 64:10.

Loki 1:04:49 Robert E. Lee was trying to change a few things here and there, and it actually reflected in his kids, as well, who did some things later in life. So, like with Brigham Young, Brigham Young is a human being, I don't know why we have this idea that prophets are perfect. Gordon B. Hinckley was like, "I'm still trying to figure all this out. I'm still trying learn." It's like, gosh, you're trying to learn? You're President Hinckley, for goodness sakes. Even in the Bible, none of the prophets are perfect, or in the Book of Mormon. So why did we feel that President Nelson, or Brigham Young or anyone else, Joseph Smith would be perfect? None of them ever said they were. I'm not a prophet, but I am entitled to the Holy Ghost, and not everything I say is inspired by the Holy Ghost. Sometimes it is, but just because I have the Holy Ghost, doesn't make me a perfect person. So, neither are the prophets. I think we have to kind of understand the context of who they are, and the times they're in. But, yes, we also can say that that was wrong. That's the other thing people kind of struggle with at times. "Well, we can't project our understanding of things now to people back then." Well, actually, we can, because right is right and wrong is wrong. We also believe in that universality of truth. People back then knew slavery was bad, and it wasn't just the people who were enslaved. After the Declaration of Independence, as we're trying to form this union, there was a big debate about this in the Constitution. Should we even have slavery? That was actually a real debate.

GT 1:06:40 Are all men equal? Apparently not.

Loki 1:06:41 Right. I mean, good grief. So, the compromise was made. Brigham Young was a racist. It doesn't mean he wasn't a prophet. It does mean he was a racist, because he was okay with this. Not every Latter-day Saint was [okay with it,] even for goodness sakes. It sounds harsh to say that. Now again, I didn't say he was a bad person. I didn't say he was a mass murderer or something like that.

Loki 1:07:20 I'm just saying he was a racist. We've had quite a few of them. Good grief. We even elect some of them. Let's just be fair.

GT 1:07:34 Sadly.

Loki 1:07:35 Yeah, and some of them are Democrats. Guess what? That's just what it is. But how we progress and how we learn how we grow. So, I think within the context of that essay, and so forth, I think personally, they hit the mark pretty well, given the fact that the Church even put something out there like that, to begin with, is pretty remarkable in dispelling a lot of these mythologies that still exist within the Church, about Cain and Abel, and the curse of Cain and these sorts of things. It's just like, what is it? *Mormon Doctrine*, the book. People still think that's doctrine, even though the opening of the book actually has a disclaimer, that says, "This is not Mormon doctrine.:

GT 1:08:21 I should do a whole podcast on that book.

Loki 1:08:26 Come on guys. It's really hard. It's really a kind of a struggle. How do you reconcile some of these things? Well, I mean, the Lord does a pretty good job with us reconciling these things. There's a high level of forgiveness that needs to exist there, and it's not easy. I'm nowhere close to that level. I actively think about it. How do we pursue that? So, I come back to my mom again, it's like, "You say these things, Mom. It's just embarrassing." You can go, "She's an old lady, and some people are just set in their ways." But she actually has a real argument for why Robert E. Lee could actually be considered a decent person.

Loki 1:09:11 I did a podcast with my mom recently on *The Uncomfortable Truth*. She said, "Robert E. Lee, he's my homeboy." I'm like, "Well, let's have that talk, Mom," because Lavaghn was on the phone, on the call as well. We'll have this conversation right now, Mom. Lavaughn goes, "Did he own people?"

"Yes."

"Was he a slaver?"

"Yes."

"Okay, that's all I need to know."

Mom's like, "Yeah, but..."

He goes, "No, no, no, that's all I want to hear. If he owned people, that's all I want to know."

That's Levaughn. He's entitled to that. Now, Mom is entitled to her opinion.

Loki 1:09:44 Part of the problem we have in society today, particularly over the past several years, is a lack of dialogue and a lack of meeting people where they are, and understanding. Do you know what? Not everyone is on the same level of understanding. It doesn't mean that you're some enlightened genius or anything. It's just that, look. People are at different stages of life. We need to meet people where they are and bring them along. That's what I tried to do when I talk about racism and so forth. Yes, sometimes I do snap at people and just shut them down immediately. But most of the time, I'm trying to have a conversation with them, because I really believe that we should [talk.]

Loki 1:10:22 The civil rights movement was about the principle of non-violence. We think of that in the physical sense, that lunch counter scene with my mom, and how they're beating on them, and so forth. But they're not fighting back. We see that constantly. [People ask,] "Well, how come you guys didn't fight back?"

"Well, we didn't want to get killed, first of all."

That technique was about survival. But that became this really iconic sort of thing about the civil rights movement, and in any sort of protest today, typically. What I talk to people about is intellectual non-violence. Let's not go to guns with people. Social media makes it really easy to do that, because, man, I can shoot back and I can get all these likes, and so forth, that dopamine effect, and whatever else. I'm like, how about intellectual non-violence where we actually have conversations. We're not shouting each other. We're talking to understand. We might agree to disagree. Well, I'm not going to agree with you, because I think you're wrong. But I want you to know where I'm at, and I know where you're at. Some people, you're just not going to change. We did a screening here in Utah of *The Uncomfortable Truth*. We had someone stand up in the middle of the film and go, "This is BS," and he walks out. Now, he was making a scene, of course, but he was also really opposed to what we were saying in the film. What did you think you were walking into, buddy? I mean, the poster should have said at all. It's like, "Did you watch the trailer?" This is at the LDS Film Festival, as a matter of fact.

GT 1:10:39 Oh, really?

Loki 1:11:48 Yeah. So, it's like, "My gosh, what did you think you were going to get?" It's fascinating to think about. I don't know, maybe I'm just wandering a little bit on that. I just think about how we really just need to [talk.] When my wife and I got sealed in the Jordan River Temple, the sealer said to me, "You have two ears and one mouth. Use them proportionately." We need to listen more and talk less. Of course, this is a podcast. I'm doing all the talking. I guess you are doing all of the listening, and your listeners are doing all of the listening. That's the whole point.

Can White People talk about Racism?

Introduction

Let's face it. Race is a tough subject to bring up. Is there ever pushback from black people when white people talk about racism? We'll talk about white people leading conversations about race with Emmy award winning director Loki Mulholland. Check out our conversation....

Interview

Loki 1:12:40 It's not a brag. It is what it is. Ruby Bridges, that little girl, that famous photo, she was in first grade. The federal marshals, and Norman Rockwell did a painting of it and so forth, she is a family friend. When we talk, and we actually did a podcast with Ruby, Levaughn, and I,[18] every time she talks, she talks about love and hate. Fundamentally, that's what it's all about. We need to find out where we stand on that, because we can't serve two masters. We need to love more and hate less.

Loki 1:13:29 Like we talked about earlier on when I did a Black Lives Matter post, or people will react to those things, and there's that level of hate that exists. When you love someone, because you're interacting with them, and you know them and you have that empathy, like the Savior has, so forth. We know we have that capacity to see people the way the Lord sees them, and we know where hate comes from. We don't want to serve that. That might not be absolute hate, but when we get worked up emotionally like that, and that emotion is to fight back, to not use intellectual non-violence, but to fire back and to say things that are hurtful, like, "all lives matter" is hurtful. I don't get to tell you how to feel, if I punch you. It's not my place as a white person to tell an African American

---

18 See https://tinyurl.com/LokiRuby

how they should feel about words, like "all lives matter." So, we need to start as Latter-day Saints to love more and hate less, quite frankly.

GT 1:14:41 That brings up another question I want to ask you about, we've talked about this on the phone before, but I think it would be good to talk about it here. I've been in some black LDS groups on Facebook, for example. A lot of times I'll try to post information about Paul Reeve[19] or Russell Stevenson,[20] historians that talk about black figures in history or issues like that. I will get a lot of pushback. "Oh, two white guys talking about race."

Loki 1:15:14 Shouldn't white people be talking about race?

GT 1:15:16 Well, that's been my response. I've actually said that. Then I get lectured that, "Well, are you publishing this in white groups?" Which, of course, I am. But a lot of times black people don't want to hear two white people. We are, even right now, two white people talking about race.

Loki 1:15:38 Yeah.

GT 1:15:40 How do you handle that? I think you've had some brush back, as well. In my mind, I just walk out of there and be like, "Okay, if you don't like my message..." I feel I'm not welcome.

Loki 1:15:51 So first, there's something you said there. Black people. No, that was a black person, not black people. That was a black person who pushed back. Not all black people push back. So, just consider the language there. We talked about this in *An Uncomfortable Truth*. Your chest starts to tighten, because we're getting attacked.

---

[19] See https://gospeltangents.com/category/paul-reeve/
[20] See https://gospeltangents.com/2018/01/29/early-life-of-elijah-ables-blackhistorymonth/

GT 1:16:21 I left that group because I was so annoyed. It wasn't just one person. I felt piled on, to be honest.

Loki 1:16:27 Well, first of all, it's social media. I mean, you also have to consider, does that person feel threatened that their messages aren't going to be heard? Do they have skin in the game, economically? Right. There's that. Trust me. There are people who, it's like, great. But, the fact of the matter is, if white people aren't talking about this, nothing's going to change.

GT 1:16:50 Right.

Loki 1:16:51 I mean, this is just to fair, because racism is a white person's disease that we keep asking everyone else to solve. Now, there's a lot of emotion involved in this, a lot more emotional investment for African Americans than it is for white people, clearly. So, that's going to come out from some people.   Again, they're entitled to those opinions. But, yeah, you can feel like you're getting piled on or whatever else, but why be in the game, if you're just going to quit?

Loki 1:17:35 People ask, "Do you ever get pushback from black people?"

I'm like, "No, most pushback that I get is actually from white people." There are some people who aren't happy with me that are African American, I'm sure. That's all right. There are African Americans who aren't happy with my mom. Good grief. That's all right. But that's not all black people, just like, not all white people are racist, for goodness sakes. It can seem like that, but not every black person is an angry black person, either.

Even though the white people, anytime a black person says something oppositional or questions somebody, [a white person might say,] "Oh, well, they're an angry black man."

I get people [that say,] "Is it unfair for you to be hired to talk about diversity inclusion? Who are you to talk about diversity inclusion."

I [respond,] "Well, [I was hired] because they're not going to listen to you, if you're black." Trust me, white people don't listen to black people. If they're talking about racism, they're definitely not listening to that. Because one, we go, "They have an agenda, because they're black." It's racism, so, of course, they have an agenda.

Loki 1:18:45 There's more of an inclination for a white person to listen to me talking about it, because also my mother. I get that little. I don't want to call it a trump card, because I don't curse. But I had that little card. I can play my mom card, because she's a civil rights activist. People can see that. There's something to be said about that. It's not for African Americans to go, "Oh, my gosh, thank goodness there's a lot of white people who are actually decent human beings," like my mother. It's for white people to go, "Oh, I didn't know we were involved in the civil rights movement. Wow." It's something to stop and think. This wasn't just a black issue. This is an American issue.

GT 1:19:31 Well, and that's what's nice about your mom, because when we think about civil rights leaders, we think about Martin Luther King, Medgar Evers, people like that, Jesse Jackson. They're always black.

Loki 1:19:41 They always will be black, by the way.

GT 1:19:42 They will. They should be. But there are white people like your mom, that have fought hard.

Loki 1:19:53 My joke was, you're talking about Dr. King and you're talking about Medgar Evers and Jesse Jackson saying they were always black. I'm like, "Well, yes, they're always black because they are black, right? But then you have my mother. Part of the problem kids have and stuff nowadays and people have when they talk about the civil rights movement is, "Oh, well, Dr. King had a dream, Rosa sat on a bus. We've arrived." That's all they see in the civil rights movement, that it's a black thing.

Loki 1:20:21 I come back to this thing, this is an American issue. This is not Black History Month, by the way, that we're recording this. This is the black experience, which is every month in American history. I've had people say, "Well, why do we have to have black history month? We don't have white History Month." I'm like, actually, we do have white History Month, it's every single month. This is not about trying to shoehorn in a white person into black history. No. So when I'm doing diversity and inclusion trainings and seminars, whatever else, talking about these things, honestly, it's because there's a better chance that someone actually might listen to what I have to say, and then they're going, "Oh, well, that wasn't too bad. I can kind of handle this a little bit." Now, they might actually be more inclined to read some of these books written by African American authors, and the like, and see these sorts of films and such, and not bristle. [They might be inclined to not] put up those walls that block that opportunity to actually listen and to empathize, at the end of the day. It's a challenge.

Loki 1:21:34 It's hard to go into a space and try to participate and get blown up for it, which is what happened to you, for example. That doesn't happen all the time, and who knows what was going on with that individual, or with those individuals in their lives? What was going on? I'd have to question going, "Okay, who was killed that day? What frustrations were they dealing with in life, and stuff that they feel that they needed to speak their mind in that fashion and question that?

Loki 1:22:11 One of the things that people say, "Well, what should I do as a white person, if I want to get involved. I say, show up and shut up. Just be there to listen, not to tell people what to do, what to think. Black people know what to think. They know what the problems are, and they know how to solve them. What we need, as a country is, the needle won't move. Luvaghn Brown talks about this. Oftentimes, in our podcast, he's like, "Look, African Americans make up what, like 12%, 14% of population. Nothing's going to change unless white people are involved." So, to make those movements happen, like Black Lives Matter, white people had to show up, because that's where the power structure is.

Loki 1:23:00 So, suddenly, now, all of a sudden, corporations are falling all over themselves to talk about Black Lives Matter. Why? Because they're seeing that actually, the people who actually buy our stuff, which is majority white people, that demographic, we want their money, and they actually care about this stuff. You need that for policy change and everything else to happen. Because, politically, that's the way the system is set up for right now. That's the space we have to operate in. But it's more about that presence, and how we can help. My mom never came into a space and said, "Hey, here's how I think it should be done." If they asked her opinion, she would tell them, if they were asking, because she was an expert. She'd already been involved in dozens of sittings and protests. Why would you not ask her? But she won't ever tell people what to do. Being at the lunch counter was an invite. Being in the Freedom Rides was an invite. It's not something we should be offended by as white people. If we're going to go and help, then, "Hey, what can I do to help?"

"Can you send an email?"

"Yeah."

"Could you staple this?"

"Sure."

We all want to be on the front lines, because that looks good for the optics and so forth. We feel good about ourselves. Click, click, get the selfies to go on Instagram, whatever else, that sort of--someone used this term the other day, I'm trying to remember it now. I would call it the social media activist, where you'll show up to a protest, just to look good. It's like, what's your real point to all of that?

Loki 1:24:42 For those who, as a white person that wants to get involved, just get involved. The most important audience is the one that you interact with, your family, or church members, whomever else. When you see, when you hear something or see something that's wrong, you say something. Don't stand back. Stand out. Step forward and call it for what it is. Believe me, it makes Elders' Quorum very interesting sometimes. I've done it. Yeah, people aren't going to be excited about you at times. But you know what? When that prompting comes to do the right thing, that's from the Spirit. We should be following the spirit. [Let's] get back to the gospel here for a moment. Yes, I'm on a tangent, but let's get back to the gospel.

GT 1:25:37 We like tangents.

Loki 1:25:41 Not everyone's excited about those sort of things, when you bring them up. But if you know the spirit is telling you to say something right when it's being said, then you need to say it. I think we think sing a hymn about that, don't we? Do what is right, let the consequence follow. Well, we didn't say do what is right when it's comfortable, when it's convenient. What's right and what's easy aren't the same thing.

Should LDS Church Apologize for Racism?

Introduction

The LDS Church prohibited black men and women from receiving priesthood rites in the temple until 1978. Should the Church apologize for past racism? Emmy award winning director Loki Mulholland will weigh in on that issue. Check out our conversation....

Interview

GT 1:26:06 You know Darron Smith,[21] don't you?

Loki 1:26:08 Yeah, he's in my film.

GT 1:26:10 Yeah. Oh, in which film?

Loki 1:26:12 *Black, White and Us.*

GT 1:26:13 Okay.

Loki 1:26:13 Yeah.

GT 1:26:14 So, I know, Darron used to teach at BYU, and he was fired, because he asked for the Church to apologize for the racial ban. What's your position on that?

Loki 1:26:30 He was fired because he was a black guy, calling [the Church] to apologize for the racial ban.

GT 1:26:38 So, do you think the Church should apologize?

---

[21] See our interview at https://gospeltangents.com/2017/04/22/racial-portrayals-of-christian-athletes/

Loki 1:26:41 Yes.

GT 1:26:41 Elder Oaks has said, "We don't seek apologies and..."[22]

Loki 1:26:46 This is not like terrorism, where we know, this is not like, hey, we don't kowtow to terrorists. We don't bribe, whatever.

GT 1:26:55 Does the Church open itself to some sort of legal liability, such as reparations for having a ban for, let's say, from 1852? Some people, Paul Reeve will quibble with me on that year, but I think that's a good place to start it, and 1978.

Loki 1:27:11 I don't know what reparations would look like, from a gospel standpoint. This isn't the ancient Catholic Church where you're paying for sins, right? It's not like, we're going to go, "Hey, you could have gotten a few more Hail Mary's in there and give them back." Or how do you give extra blessings for missed opportunities for going to the temple and so forth? It's not like you're going to get [extra blessings.] You're not checking off a box for like, "Yeah, I think I deserve 20 more extra endowment sessions, even though I didn't go. I want that on my record, so people know." Believe it or not, the Church already is doing work and reparations, in the respect of the work that they're putting forth and the resources for the Freedmen's Bureau and so forth, and the economic help that they're providing in cooperation with NAACP and doing these things. It might not be the reparations people want to see. But I think there is something there, by the way. But what's the harm in apologizing? This is a political issue at that point. So, the reason the U.S. doesn't apologize for slavery is because then that makes them accountable. Congress doesn't apologize, because once you do, then you recognize that you're actually accountable. Well, don't we actually believe in fixing mistakes? Don't we actually believe in that sort of stuff? Isn't that the whole principle of the Gospel?

____

[22] See https://archive.sltrib.com/article.php?id=2122123&itype=cmsid

GT 1:28:40 Elder Oaks doesn't, apparently.

Loki 1:28:45 First, you have to recognize it as a sin. So, a wrong was done. President Oaks is a lawyer, so let's just be fair. We all know that. I don't mean to say anything bad about lawyers or President Oaks. At the end of the day, if a wrong was done, then yes, we need to apologize for that wrong. Then, okay, well, how do we fix that? What does that look like? Sometimes it's just an apology. There's nothing wrong with apologizing, even if you don't think you're wrong. If someone else was injured, you might not have meant it. That's not what your intent was, but you apologize for some of the simplest things. In this regard, why not apologize? I just don't understand why that wouldn't be the case. We've pretty much come out and said this wasn't a Church policy, but we allowed it to continue. My understanding is there's no written document anywhere saying that blacks shouldn't have the priesthood. There was nothing at the proverbial pulpit, if you will, in General Conference. There are no words from the prophets that says black shouldn't have the priesthood. There's no declaration.

GT 1:30:09 Just that 1852 sermon or not sermon. It was before the state legislature, but there was a statement made by Brigham Young that "I will not allow blacks to rule over me."

Loki 1:30:19 Right. But that's not a Church statement. That's a legislative statement.

GT 1:30:23 Exactly.

Loki 1:30:24 That's two different things, maybe not in Utah.

GT 1:30:29 It was a theocracy in Utah.

Loki 1:30:30 At the end of the day, it's like, Look. A wrong is a wrong, so just apologize for that wrong. I mean, there's only good things that can come from that. You might actually have to eat a little crow or something, or whatever it is. But, at the end of the day, look how much more the blessings are going to come from that, that people aren't going to hold that over you anymore. I just don't see the problem in apologizing, I guess. At the end of the day, it'll come in all around. I just don't see the problem with that.

GT 1:31:08 Yeah. It's doing what is right, and letting the consequences follow.

Loki 1:31:12 Yeah, we practice what we preach.

GT 1:31:13 That's our hymn.

Loki 1:31:16 Maybe there is something for Darron Smith in all of that in regards of, look, you got fired for something he should have been fired for, so maybe there's reparations for him in that regard. If other people were impacted, because they couldn't get certain jobs within the Church, because they didn't have the priesthood, or they didn't have a temple recommend. There are certain positions in the Church in regards, at Church headquarters and so forth, where you need to be an active member of the Church and this, that and this, whatever else. Maybe that's changed, I don't know. Okay, well, then some people were excluded from that, what does that look like?

Loki 1:31:53 Reparations doesn't necessarily mean you're doling out cash to people. are certain institutions like Georgetown University that sold people. The Jesuit Church there that sold people to pay for the school and stuff. They were kind of in financial straits. "Well, let's sell some of our enslaved people so we can pay the bills." I mean, good grief. What are they doing now? They're providing education to the descendants of those people that they held as slaves. That's a form of reparation.

Loki 1:32:27 What could we be doing from an education standpoint, for example, at Brigham Young University, or any of our educational institutions to help that imbalance? If we believe that education is the key to the future and so forth. There are different ways that look at that. I have no problem with an apology. I think it'd be a great thing to do. That's not just because Darron Smith, is a friend of mine. But, look at the impact that's had on Darron Smith, in his attitudes toward the Church.

GT 1:33:09 Because he's no longer active, right?

Loki 1:33:10 Yeah, he's not. He's not an active member right now. But that could have been different. What does the scripture, say, in the D&C, about, even just one soul?[23] Well, there's one soul. There'll all important in the eyes of God. They should all be important to us. That should be a reason enough alone, quite frankly. Now, compound that by the hundreds of thousands of souls that have been impacted because of a lack of an apology or a lack of empathy. And by not apologizing, the attitudes [aren't what they should be] that exist amongst white members, who didn't think that was that big of a deal, who don't understand what that means and looks like. [We should] mourn with those who mourn. It's that trickle-down effect, and it takes time. We are not a fast-moving church, to say the least, and that's good and bad. Of course, to some people, when we do make a statement, oh, again, we come back to this idea is like, "Oh, there's been prophets--there's being with the times." We should probably be more with the times than not, but in a way that I think we're seeing more and more in the Church of this coming back around to the idea that we're followers of Jesus Christ. That means we actually believe in what he said and that we should treat each other the way we want to be treated.

---

[23] D&C 18:15-16: "15 And if it so be that you should labor all your days in crying repentance unto this people, and bring, save it be one soul unto me, how great shall be your joy with him in the kingdom of my Father!

16 And now, if your joy will be great with one soul that you have brought unto me into the kingdom of my Father, how great will be your joy if you should bring many souls unto me!"

Loki 1:34:50 When the Church comes out and says things about racism, when they come out and say things about caging children, illegals. When they're [the government is] caging human beings and they're [the Church is] calling wrong, wrong. That's progress. I get excited about that. It doesn't mean there's not other things we can't be getting better about. They are talking about LGBTQ issues and suicide and all these other things that are real. These are real things. Now, if you're homophobic or racist, or whatever else, xenophobic, that's on you. Maybe this isn't the Church for you. Otherwise, repent, and go, "You know what? Okay. Clearly, this is a message that the Church, that Heavenly Father believes is important for us to hear." So, we need to be preaching this a lot more, and converting souls unto Christ in more ways than one. We need to be converting the souls that are within the Church, to Christ. I love what he's preaching. I'm not perfect at it. But, in my little space, that's what I try to do with the films and the work that I do is to help end racism and to bring the pass the immortality and the eternal life of man through that.

GT 1:36:18 Great. Well, any last thoughts you want to share with us before I let you go? We've been here for a couple hours, so, I appreciate your time.

Loki 1:36:26 Yeah, and the Church says, amen. I don't know. I don't have any more thoughts. I can keep talking forever. When my mom speaks and stuff, they're like, "Well, how long can she speak for?" I'm like, "Well, how long do you want her to speak for?" I can ramble on forever, just like my mom. There's a lot to be said, we're just scratching the surface.

GT 1:36:48 You've got a couple of websites. Why don't you tell us what those are?

Loki 1:36:51 Well, LokiMulholland.com. That's my personal website where you can get the blog and some of the videos and the like, and if you want me to come and speak. No one ever asks me to do firesides. That's fascinating. I don't know why.

GT 1:37:04 Me neither.

Loki 1:37:06 I speak all over the country, but not firesides. There's jtmfoundation.org, which is our Foundation's website.

Loki 1:37:15 Joan Trumpauer Mulholland, yeah, but jtmfoundation.org. We're doing a lot of work, a lot of good work in this realm.

GT 1:37:15 Joan Trumpauer.

GT 1:37:28 What's the website for your podcast?

Loki 1:37:32 It's called, *The Uncomfortable Truth.* There's not a website for it.

GT 1:37:34 Oh, it's not a website?

Loki 1:37:35 You can go to my you can go to lokimulholland.com, and the podcast is on there as well.

GT 1:37:39 Okay.

Loki 1:37:39 It feeds in from Anchor. But, it's on all the major platforms, Spotify, Amazon, wherever.

GT 1:37:45 So just search for *The Uncomfortable Truth.*

Loki 1:37:47 Yeah, in your favorite platform. Yeah. You're either going to get very angry or you're going to get very enlightened.

GT 1:37:55 Or maybe both.

Loki 1:37:58 If it's uncomfortable, that's probably good. That's the Spirit talking to you.

GT 1:38:02 I love your tagline. Let's get uncomfortable.

Loki 1:38:04 Yeah.

GT 1:38:07 All right. Well, Loki Mulholland, I really appreciate you being here on *Gospel Tangents,* and it's great to have been such a good friend for the past decade and a half.

Loki 1:38:16 Yeah, I can't believe it's taken you this long to get me on your show. That's not because of me. It probably is, I've been very busy.

GT 1:38:24 (Chuckling) Well, and I encourage everybody to watch that latest [film, *The End of Slavery*.] It's only 21 minutes.

Loki 1:38:30 Yes, it's a short, 21 minutes, *The End of Slavery: the Fight for Amendment C.*

GT 1:38:34 It's on Amazon.

Loki 1:38:35 It's on Amazon. Yeah, the *End of Slavery* and *The Evers*, which is 90 minutes, but Wow. Most people say that's my best film yet.

GT 1:38:44 Oh, yeah. I haven't been able to see it yet, but I've been looking forward to it.

Loki 1:38:48 I appreciate it. Thank you so much.

GT 1:38:49 Thanks.

Additional Resources:

Check out our other interviews about racism with Dr. Darron Smith.

Darron Smith on Race, Religion, & Sport

Dr. Darron Smith, teaches Sociology & Public Health at University of Memphis,

035: Overcoming "Nice" Racism

034: BYU Protests

033: How do Minorities fare at BYU?

032: True & False Rape Allegations at BYU

031: How BYU Could Improve the Honor Code for Black Students

030: Black Graduation Rates at BYU

Mark Staker on First Black Mormon: Black Pete

Dr. Mark Staker, Ph.D in anthropology, LDS Church History Library

Margaret Young on Jane Manning James

Rick Bennett, Darius Gray, and Margaret Young

Dr. Paul Reeve on Black Mormon History in Utah

Dr. Paul Reeve – Prof of History, University of Utah.

Russell Stevenson – Biographer of Elijah Abel

Dr. Russell Stevenson, Biographer of Elijah Ables

Newell Bringhurst – Author of Saints, Slaves, and Blacks

Dr. Newell Bringhurst, author of several books on Mormon History

Matt Harris – Black History WW2 to Present

Dr. Matt Harris, History Professor, CSU-Pueblo

David Ostler: Building Bridges to Questioners

David Ostler has a new book called "Bridges: Ministering to Those Who Question"

Quincy Newell: Biographer of Jane Manning James

Dr. Quincy Newell, Hamilton College discusses her biography of Black Mormon Pioneer Jane Manning James.

Race Struggles at BYU 1965-1985

Dr. Matt Harris discusses the LDS race ban 1965-1985

Critiquing the LDS Gospel Topics Essays

Dr. Newell Bringhurst (left) & Dr. Matt Harris are co-editors of "The LDS Gospel Topics Series."

458: Race, Priesthood, & Randy Bott

457: Racism in Mormon Scripture

456: Pros & Cons of Race Essay

Changing LDS Messages for Blacks, Feminists, Gays

Dr. Taylor Petrey's book, "Tabernacles of Clay," outlines changing messages from LDS Church leaders over the past 70 years on blacks, gays, and feminists.

433: LDS Leaders on Interracial Marriage

Breaking Racial Barriers: Joseph Freeman & LDS Priesthood

Joseph Freeman was first black man ordained after 1978 revelation on priesthood.

495: #BlackLivesMatter

494: Enduring Systemic Racism

493: Genesis Group & Black Spirituality

492: Instant Celebrity

491: Joseph's Baptism

490: Meeting Mormons at PCC

489: Holiness Preacher Joins Army

Final Thoughts

You can get our transcripts at our amazon.com author page. I've got a link here, but just do a search for Gospel Tangents interview, and you should be able to find a bunch of them there. Please subscribe at Patreon.com/gospeltangents. For $5 a month, you can hear the entire interview uncut and for $10 you can get a pdf copy. We've also got a $15 tier where if you want a physical copy, I'll be the first to send it to you, so please subscribe at Patreon or on our website at Gospeltangents.com. For our latest updates, please like our page at facebook.com/Gospeltangents and also check our twitter updates Gospel tangents. Please subscribe on our apple podcast page tinyurl.com/GospelTangents, or you can subscribe on your android device. Just do a search for Gospel Tangents. Thanks again for listening. Click here to subscribe, here for transcript and over here we've got some more of our great videos. Thanks again.